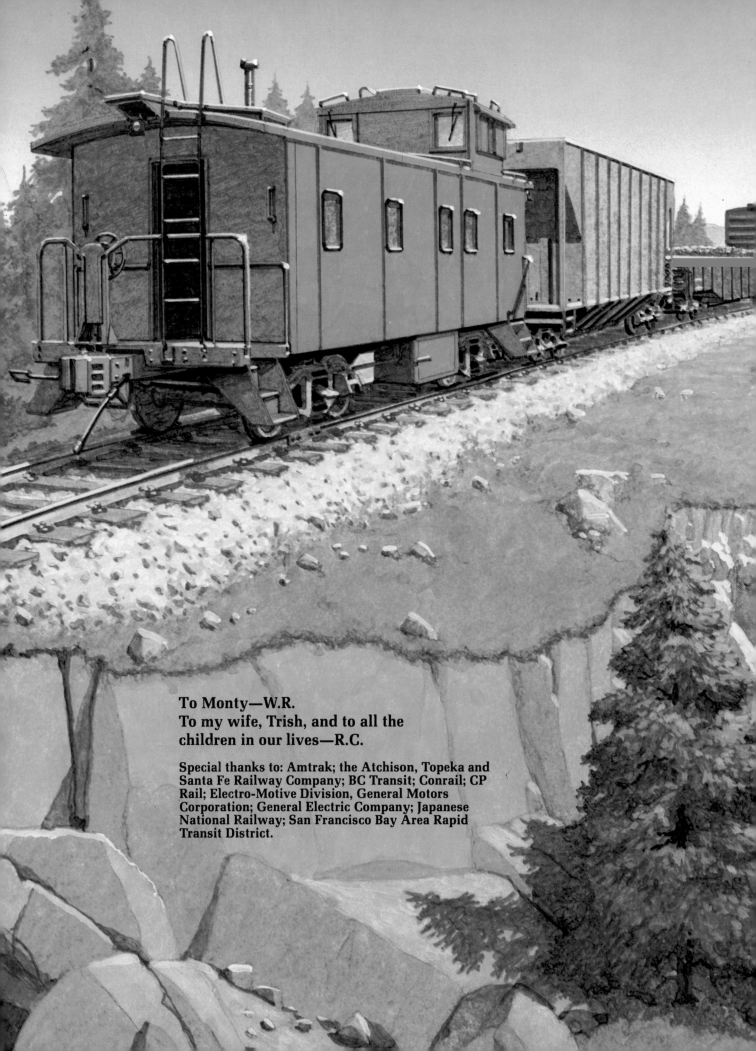

To Monty—W.R.
To my wife, Trish, and to all the
children in our lives—R.C.

Special thanks to: Amtrak; the Atchison, Topeka and
Santa Fe Railway Company; BC Transit; Conrail; CP
Rail; Electro-Motive Division, General Motors
Corporation; General Electric Company; Japanese
National Railway; San Francisco Bay Area Rapid
Transit District.

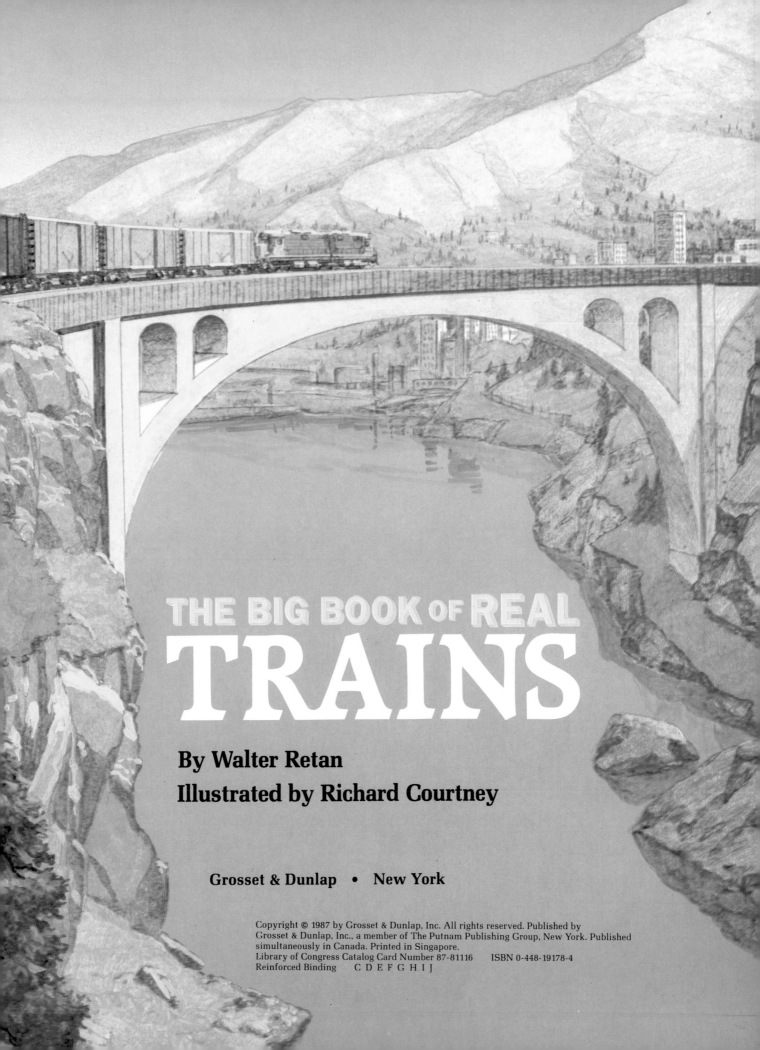

THE BIG BOOK OF REAL
TRAINS

By Walter Retan

Illustrated by Richard Courtney

Grosset & Dunlap • New York

Library of Congress Catalog Card Number 87-81116   ISBN 0-448-19178-4
Reinforced Binding   C D E F G H I J

Until the invention of the locomotive, few people could travel farther than the next village or the nearest city. All trips over land had to be made on foot or horseback, or in a stagecoach or wagon. Long journeys took weeks—even months. Many people died from hunger or exhaustion. The locomotive changed all that. Railroads became the world's first form of quick, cheap land transportation. They brought countries and people together in a way that had never before been possible.

Steam Locomotives are some of the most amazing machines in the world. For more than a hundred years they pulled nearly all of the trains that ran on railroads throughout the world. When one of these giant steam monsters chugged into a station and slowed to a stop, a shiver of excitement ran through everyone waiting on the platform. When the locomotive pulled out again, the whistle blasted, the bell clanged, and smoke and steam began to escape into the air. Passengers could hear a steady *choo-choo-choo* as the wheels began to turn faster and faster.

The Golden Age of Railroads

The very first trains ran on wooden rails. Horses were used to pull open carts loaded with coal from the mines to a river or canal. There the coal was loaded on to a boat. Without the smooth wooden rails, the wheels of the heavy carts would have sunk into the mud when rain flooded the dirt roads.

The English were the first to try building a locomotive driven by a steam engine. In 1829, George Stephenson built the first really successful steam locomotive—the **Rocket.** It ran on smooth rails and had a tall chimney that looked like a stove pipe.

In America, an inventor named Peter Cooper built a steam locomotive called **Tom Thumb.** He wanted the owners of the new Baltimore and Ohio Railroad to use steam locomotives instead of horses to pull their trains. In 1830, the railroad owner suggested a race to prove that horses were faster than locomotives. At first **Tom Thumb** led the race. But then a belt on the engine broke and the little locomotive slowed to a stop. The horse won!

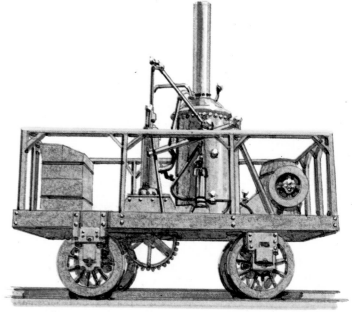

By 1850, American trains were chugging through the countryside. The passenger cars were simply stagecoaches with special wheels for staying on the rails. Even today, passenger cars are called coaches.

In 1869, the first railroad across the western part of the United States was finished. (Trains from the east were already running as far west as the Mississippi River.) The Central Pacific Railroad laid the rails eastward from California, while the Union Pacific laid tracks westward from Nebraska. They met in Utah, where an official from each company hammered a golden spike that completed the railroad.

In 1925, the first commercial diesel-electric locomotive was put into service in New Jersey. Though nobody realized it, the diesel engine would one day end the reign of the steam locomotive. The monster engines burned too much fuel, wasted much of the heat they produced, and needed constant attention.

Train and Track Facts

Trains run on a set of steel rails fastened to crossties underneath. The ties hold the track together and keep the rails an equal distance apart. In the United States, ties are usually made of wood to cushion the rails. The rails are joined end to end by pieces of steel called fishplates. The fishplates cause the *click-clack* sound that is heard when the train wheels run along the rails. Today rails are often welded together to make a smoother, safer ride.

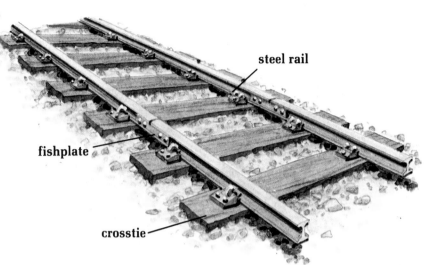

steel rail

fishplate

crosstie

Trains roll along on a special kind of wheel called a flanged wheel. The flange is a rim on the inner edge of the wheel, guiding the locomotive or car along the track. Because of the flange, trains don't have to be steered like cars or trucks or ships.

flange wheel

Cars on early trains were held together by chains. When the train stopped, each car crashed into the one in front of it. The invention of the automatic coupler put an end to this problem. When the cars come together, they join automatically. The two parts of the coupler grip each other like two fists. There is always an equal distance between the cars, whether they are moving along the tracks or jolting to a stop.

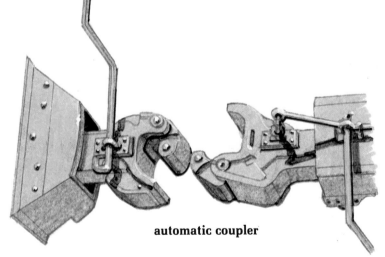

automatic coupler

How a Steam Locomotive Runs

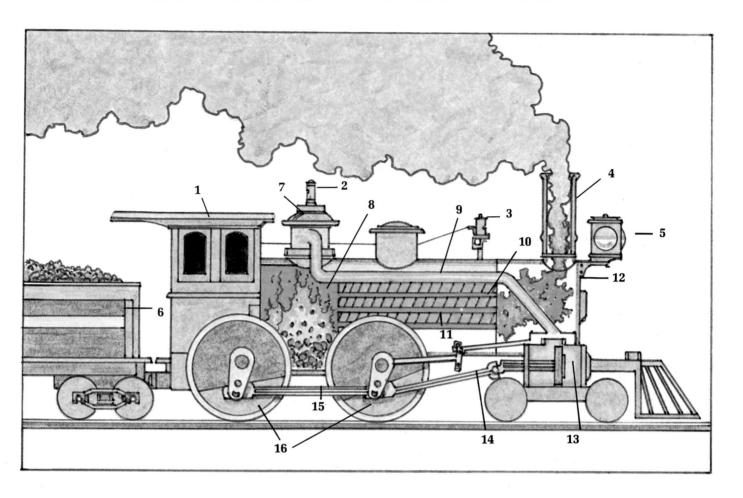

1. cab	5. headlight	9. steam pipe	13. piston
2. whistle	6. tender	10. boiler tubes	14. drive rod
3. bell	7. steam dome	11. water	15. connecting rod
4. smokestack	8. firebox	12. smoke box	16. driving wheels

A **Steam Locomotive** burns coal—or sometimes fuel oil—in a firebox. The heat turns the water in the boiler into steam. The pressure produced by the steam forces it into the steam dome, and from there through the steam pipe to the cylinders. Inside the cylinders, the pressure of the steam moves the piston back and forth. As the piston moves, the drive rod and connecting rod also move. This turns the driving wheels. The *choo-choo* sound you hear when a steam locomotive chugs down the track is the sound of steam pushing the piston first in one direction and then another. Attached directly behind the locomotive is a car or compartment called a tender. It holds the fuel and sometimes extra water.

Diesel-Electric Locomotives have almost entirely replaced steam locomotives on major freight rail lines in the United States. They are cheaper to operate. They can supply their own power, so they are able to run wherever there are rails. They can also make long runs without refueling or servicing. A diesel locomotive is often made up of several connecting units. An A unit can be used by itself; it contains an engineer's cab and the controls needed to serve as a lead unit. B units support the A unit. They provide extra power without the need for an extra crew. The engineer in the lead unit controls the B units by radio signals from his cab. These support units can be placed anywhere in the train.

How Diesel Power Works

The diesel engine in a locomotive is similar to the one in a big trailer-truck. It works by compressing, or squeezing, air in chambers called cylinders. (Most locomotive diesel engines have 12-16 cylinders.) In each cylinder, air is compressed by a piston and the temperature rises. This rise in temperature sets fire to the fuel oil that has been injected into the cylinder. This produces the power to drive an electric generator. The electric generator turns the drive wheels and the locomotive moves.

1

air

piston   cylinder

2

fuel oil

Hopper Cars carry loose loads that can be dumped or poured into the top of the car and unloaded through chutes at the bottom. Coal, gravel, sand, or grain are good examples of the kind of cargo hopper cars usually haul. They have high sides and ends. The ends slant sharply toward the center, causing the cargo to move down and fall out of the bottom as soon as the chutes are opened.

Covered hopper cars carry freight, like grain or salt, that needs protection from the weather. Open-top hoppers haul freight like ore, coal, or gravel. A long freight train of open-top hopper cars can be loaded—one car at a time—as the cars pass underneath an automatic loading tower. To unload, the cars are pulled up an elevated ramp. As each car reaches the top, its chutes are opened. The load falls into storage bins located below the ramp.

Gondolas are among the most useful cars on a freight train. These cars look like long metal boxes on wheels. Gondola cars usually carry heavy, bulky loads like steel pipes, cement blocks, and containers filled with goods. Some of these cars have hinged ends or sides for unloading. Others are unloaded by special dumping machines that can jack up the gondola and tilt it over on its side so that the cargo slides out easily.

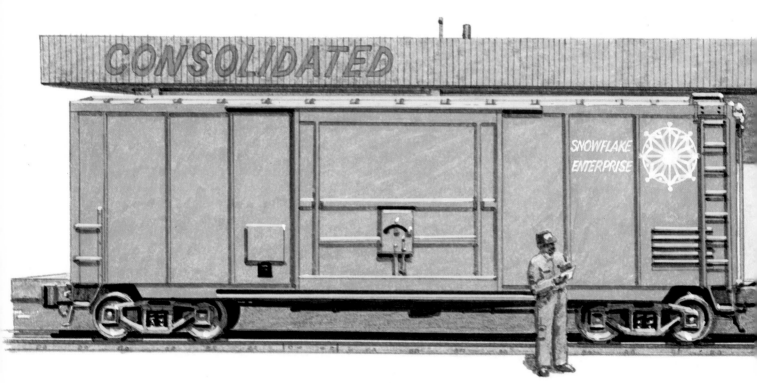

Refrigerator Cars carry products that must be kept cool or frozen, such as meat, fruit, and vegetables. The first refrigerator cars were cooled by fans blowing air over ice. Today these special boxcars have their own refrigerator units. The sides of many of these cars are built of two layers of steel with insulation between. Sometimes there is a foamlike kind of insulation on the outside.

Livestock Cars are used to haul cattle, sheep, pigs, and even chickens to market. The cars have open-slatted siding. The slats let in fresh air to keep the animals cool and help them breathe.

There are also troughs for feed and water, and clean straw or sand to cover the floor. Some livestock cars have double decks for sheep and pigs and other smaller animals.

Boxcars look like windowless boxes on wheels. There are more boxcars than any other kind of railway car. Originally, boxcars were made of wood. Now they are built from steel. There is at least one big sliding door on each side so cargo can be loaded and unloaded. Boxcars carry all kinds of general freight—from television sets to canned goods, to clothing—anything that needs protection from the weather.

Flatcars are open platforms on wheels. They can carry almost anything—from logs to military tanks. Strong chains and ropes anchor the cargo securely to the platform. Sometimes tall stakes line the sides, giving extra protection. There are many special kinds of flatcars. One with a sunken center is used for moving huge pieces of equipment such as heavy construction machinery. Without a sunken center, the cargo might stand too high for it to go under bridges and through tunnels.

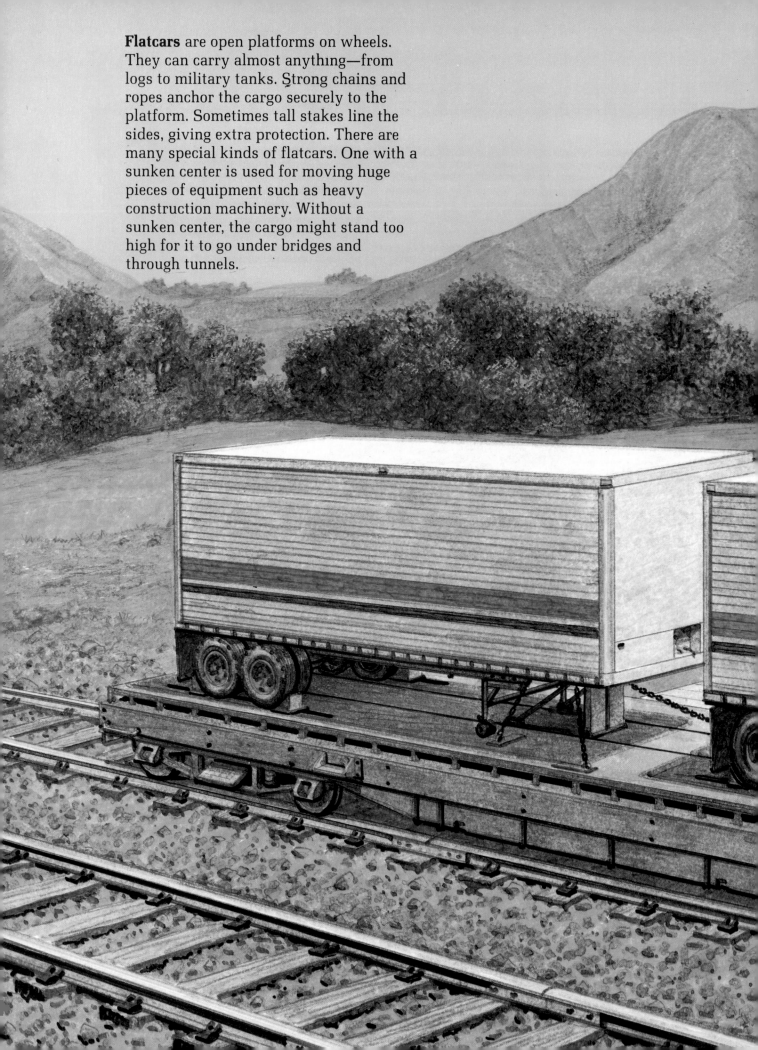

A **Piggyback Flatcar** can carry two giant truck trailers. The train hauls the trailers, fully loaded, across the country. When the trailers are taken off the train, truck drivers attach them to tractors for local delivery. In West Germany there is even a "piggyback" train that carries *both* the tractor and the trailer. This train also includes a special "dormitory" car for the drivers, who travel with their trucks. When the train arrives in Italy, the trailer-trucks are unloaded, and the drivers deliver them to their destinations.

Tank Cars are really big steel tanks traveling on wheels. They carry all kinds of liquids, including fuel oil, gasoline, fish oil, orange juice, milk, and turpentine. These big metal cans that travel on their sides have different kinds of linings according to their cargo. Milk tanks have to have a glass or steel lining. Liquid chemicals require a rubber, aluminum, or lead lining. Specially reinforced tank cars carry gases under high pressure; others are filled with powdered materials. There are more than 100 kinds of tank cars.

Tank cars are loaded through valves at the top of the tank car and unloaded through outlets at the bottom. Some cars may have more than one compartment. The compartments must be full so that a cargo like milk doesn't slosh around. (It might churn itself into butter!) Milk has to be kept cool. But a cargo of lard (a kind of cooking fat) has to be kept warm by special heating coils so that it doesn't become too firm or hard. A tank car carrying fuel oil frequently empties its cargo into a tanker-trailer. Then the oil can be delivered to points that the railroad doesn't reach.

Auto-Rack Cars carry brand-new automobiles directly from the factory to delivery points around the country. The auto-rack carrier is just another special version of the basic flatcar. Some cars have a two-tier framework; others have three tiers. A three-tier carrier can hold as many as 12 standard-sized or 18 subcompact autos. Each year these special cars carry more than half of the new automobiles that are delivered in cities around the country.

A unique metal framework added to the flatcar permits the loading of these new autos on two or three different levels. At each end of the tier there is a pair of platform-like structures. These can be raised or lowered. When they are lowered to match the platforms on the next car, they form a bridge. Because of these bridges, the automobiles can be driven from car to car at any level.

A **Caboose** is a railroad car that was once at the end of every freight train. It served as an office for the conductor as well as a "home" for the crew. The caboose contained a desk for the conductor, bunks, lockers, a stove, and storage space for flags, lanterns, and emergency tools. There was also a telephone so the crew could talk to the engineer at the front of the train. On long trips the crew cooked meals in the caboose, while the conductor sat at his desk checking his freight lists and delivery points.

The caboose often had a raised watchtower, or cupola, on the roof, where the rear brakeman, or conductor, could watch the moving train and look out for signals from the crew. Today there is little need for cabooses on freight trains. Computers are used to help run trains, check cargo, keep track of cars, and perform many other duties. As a result, most U.S. states have done away with laws that require cabooses on freight trains.

The Freight Yard

Every day at least 1,000 freight trains travel through the United States. On the average these trains pull between 65 and 70 cars each. Some may pull as many as 200. Often the cars in these trains are mixed. A train may start as a unit in Los Angeles, but some of the cars may be headed for Des Moines, others for New Orleans, and still others for Boston. How do the railroads keep track of these cars? How do the trainmasters in freight yards across the country see that each car gets attached to the correct locomotive at the right location? How do the cars arrive at their proper destinations?

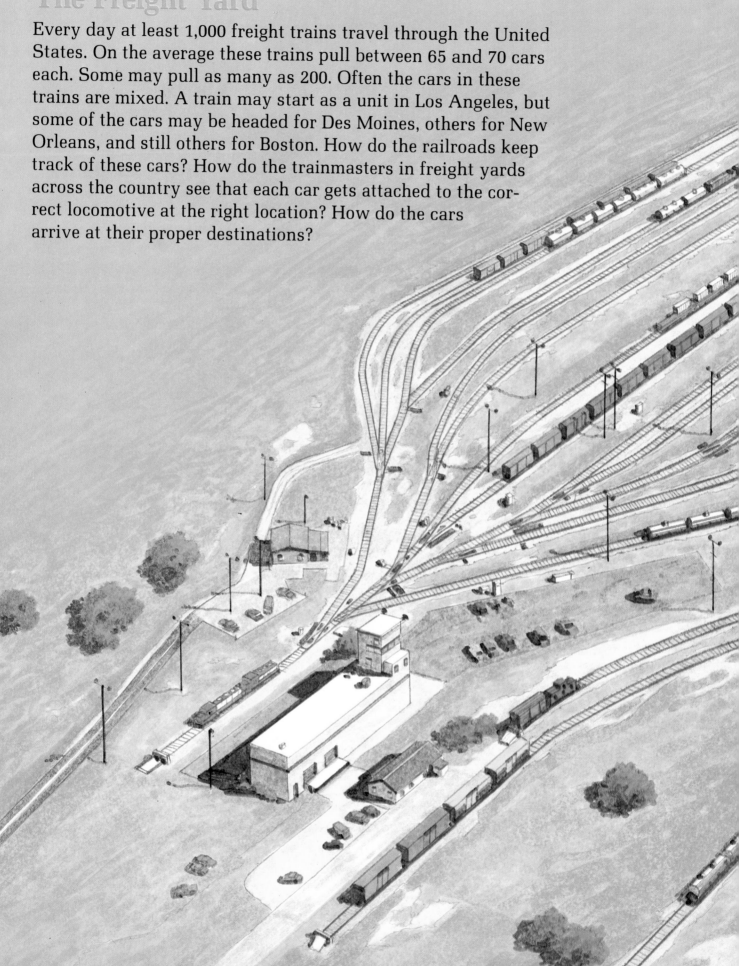

The answer is simple. A freight yard has three main parts: **1** A **receiving area** where the complete train enters. **2** A **classification yard** where cars are separated and sorted so they can be attached to new trains. **3** A **departure yard** where newly sorted trains leave for the next step of the journey.

The classification yard has a large number of parallel tracks. Each track is set aside for cars assigned to a particular route. An arriving train approaches the yard along a main track. Then a special locomotive called a switch engine pushes the cars up a small hill called the "hump." From a single track—at the far end of the hump—the parallel tracks spread out like a huge fan.

The **Hump** speeds up the work of classifying cars. One by one, as each car climbs the hump in the classification yard, it is detached from the cars behind it. In newer hump yards a computer operator electronically opens the switch that will lead the car onto the proper set of tracks. Gravity does the rest. The car rolls down the hill and automatically couples with the cars already waiting on the track.

Some hump yards are older and there railway workmen handle most of this job: setting switches, braking cars, coupling them together, and much more. Today electronic equipment makes it possible for a single operator to run a whole freight yard just by pushing buttons on his control panel in the hump control tower.

Hump Control Tower

Cars On Main Track

To Classification Tracks ➡

A scanner "reads" the color-coded label that identifies each car and its contents.

Close-up of the color-coded identification label.

Retarders control the speed of each car down the hill.

Freight Train and Yard Crews

A **conductor** supervises the train's operation and takes care of the freight paperwork.

An **engineer** operates the locomotive.

Brakemen uncouple cars, help with the signaling, and perform other jobs.

A **yardmaster** supervises the railroad yard.

A **switchman** assists in moving cars in a railroad yard.

A **train dispatcher** oversees the departure of trains from the railroad yard.

A **signalman** manages the signal box, which controls trains entering a specific section of the rail network.

Track repair gangs make sure the track is in good condition by replacing old rails and ties.

Piggyback Freight Shipments

To compete with trucks for freight business, railroads developed the idea of intermodal—or piggyback—freight shipments. This system combines the best features of water, motor, and rail shipping. Truck trailers and steamship containers can be loaded onto special flatcars for shipment by rail. (A container looks like a truck trailer without the wheels.) Once a destination is reached, the goods—still in containers—can be shifted to trucks for local delivery.

For instance, the Santa Fe Railroad can pick up freight containers from a ship docked at the Los Angeles port and carry them by rail to Chicago. There, the cars can quickly be transferred to Conrail tracks for delivery on the East Coast. Many companies own their own truck trailers—and some even own their own ships. They have also developed amazing new lifts and cranes for unloading and transferring heavy trailers and containers. Once again trains are competing successfully with trucks for freight business.

Electric Locomotives are different from steam and diesel engines. Electric locomotives don't produce their own power. They get it from a central power plant that may be a long distance away. A special overhead cable or a third rail alongside the track transfers power to the locomotive.

Electric locomotives have many advantages. They can draw huge amounts of power from a central power plant. Diesel and steam engines

Power pickup by means of overhead cable and pantagraph on locomotive.

Power pickup from center third rail.

Power pickup from side third rail.

are limited to the power they can produce themselves. Electric locomotives are also very quiet. Because they don't produce any smoke or unpleasant exhaust gases, they are especially useful for pulling trains in and around cities. They are also good for underground tracks or for traveling through long tunnels. Today electric locomotives pull a large number of the high-speed passenger trains in many parts of the world.

Coaches are the cars most commonly used on passenger trains. Usually they have rows of seats on both sides of an open aisle running through the center of the car. Today about three-quarters of all U.S. rail passengers ride in coaches on suburban commuter trains. These are the short-distance passenger trains that travel between the center of a big city like New York or Chicago and the smaller cities and towns in the suburbs. A coach on a commuter train is not built for comfort. It is built to carry as many passengers as possible (about 50 to 90). These short-distance trains do an outstanding job of cutting down on the traffic flowing through crowded city streets. Passengers on only one commuter train might require as many as 1,000 automobiles to carry them to work.

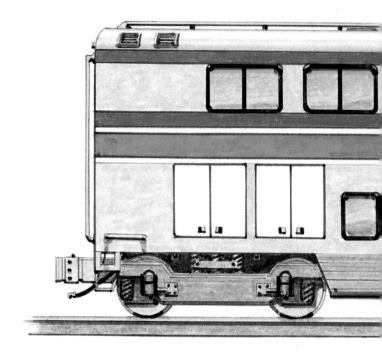

Coaches on long-distance trains are usually more comfortable. The seats have arm rests and there is plenty of leg room. It is possible to read, nap, look out the window, or walk around and stretch. Some special trains even have reclining seats equipped with drop-down trays and overhead lighting.

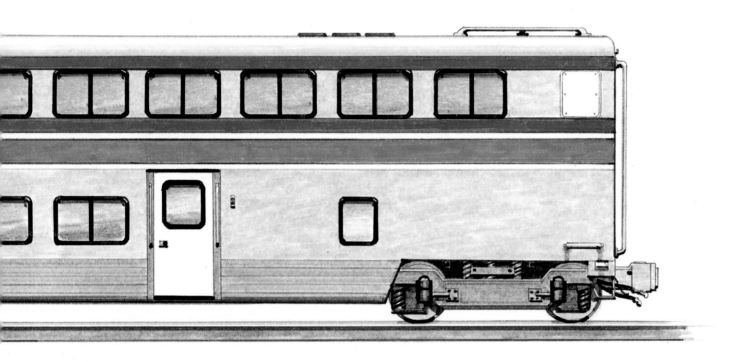

Observation Cars and **Lounge Cars** are often included in long-distance trains. Passengers can sit in the upper deck of the Vista-Dome cars and enjoy the passing scenery while they chat. Instead of facing front, the seats face the large panoramic windows. In lounge cars, passengers sit at tables and have light refreshments or play cards.

Dining Cars are restaurants on wheels. From the outside, a dining car looks very much like a coach. Inside, a row of tables and chairs runs down each side of the car. Most dining cars—or diners, as they are often called—serve breakfast, lunch, and dinner on a long trip. The food is prepared in a kitchen that sometimes occupies one end of the diner, or can be in an adjoining car. Waiters serve the food from trays, and there are menus to show the selection of food items passengers can order.

On some trains waiters serve meals to passengers at their seats. A drop-down tray fastened to the back of the seat in front pulls down to hold the meal, just as on an airplane. In other trains, there is only a cafe or snack car. The food is usually served from a counter. Travelers can order light meals, snacks, and beverages from the attendant. There may be a few tables to eat from or simply shelves and counters. Passengers also can buy a snack and carry it back to a coach seat.

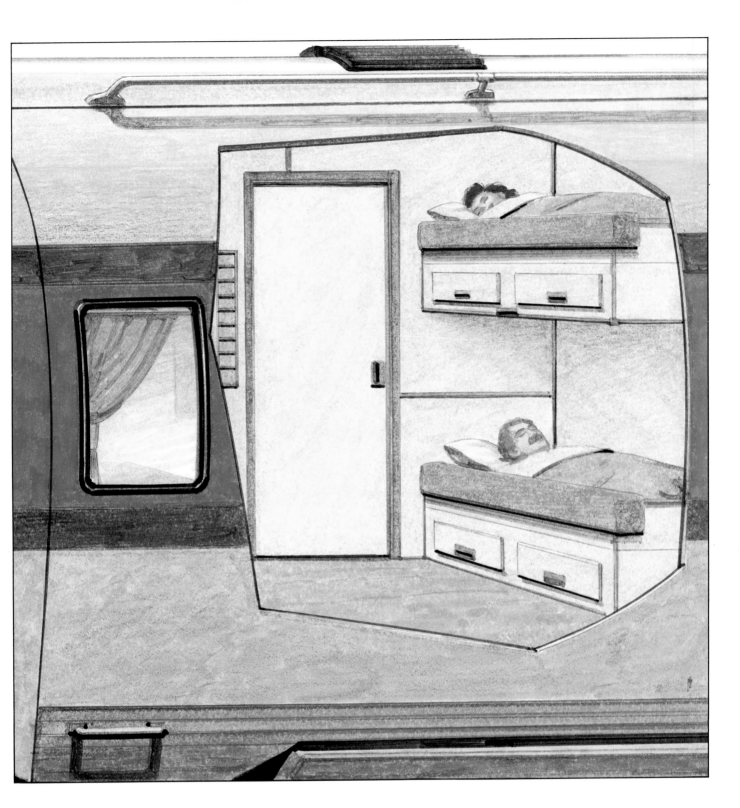

Sleeping Cars turn the train into a hotel at night. The passengers can have a deluxe private bedroom or an economy slumbercoach. Sleeping cars also include private toilets and washrooms. Sometimes a comfortable daytime coach seat turns into a bed at night. Other times the bed folds down from the wall. Some trains have family bedrooms that provide plenty of seating during the day and two full-size beds and two children's beds at night.

On some first-class trains such as the Metroliner, which runs from New York to Washington D.C., passengers can board the train during the evening, get into bed whenever they please, and awake to find that they have reached the end of their trip. Metroliners are the fastest passenger trains in the United States. They travel about 80 miles an hour, but can go much faster if the tracks are in good condition.

The **Shinkansen** is the most famous high-speed train line of the Japanese National Railway (JNR), which boasts that you can set your watch by JNR trains. They are fast and they run on time. Because of their sleek, streamlined appearance, the Shinkansen expresses are called "bullet trains." They look like some kind of futuristic dragons as they roar past with bright twin headlights and white conelike noses.

The Shinkansen trains are almost totally automatic. They are operated by remote control from computer centers in Tokyo and Osaka. The engineer in the cab of the train takes care of whatever small amount of hand operation the train needs. The track, built especially for the train, is elevated to eliminate going up and down hills. The construction of the special tracks and the electric power plants for running the trains cost a lot of money. The results have been well worth the expense. Passenger fares more than pay for the operating costs. The Shinkansen line has a good safety record. Cars are carefully inspected after every 19,000 miles of operation, and the track is checked at least every ten days.

The **"Oranges"** is the nickname given to the popular streamlined, bright-orange trains that run between the French cities of Paris and Lyon. The French are very proud of their modern passenger trains. They have good reason to be. These trains are fast enough to compete with airplanes. On the "Oranges" the landscape flies by at speeds of more than 150 miles per hour! The double tracks with welded rails and concrete ties are totally new. Only passenger trains are allowed to run on them. Heavy freight trains would quickly beat the tracks out of the delicate alignment

necessary for smooth, high-speed passenger travel. After the French National Railroad introduced its record-breaking "Orange" trains, the airlines had to cut their service between Paris and Lyon by half!

In late 1989 an even faster train started running between Paris and the French Atlantic coast. The **T.G.V. Atlantique**—with its shiny silver and blue cars—can travel at speeds up to 223 miles an hour. These new trains have telephones, compartments for business meetings, and nurseries where passengers can warm baby bottles and change diapers.

Subways are underground railroads. The trains run through tunnels bored, or cut, beneath city streets and buildings. They carry passengers through the business section of the city, as well as to and from their homes. Subway travel is fast, direct, and cheap. It helps keep city streets from getting clogged up with too many cars. It also cuts down on the amount of exhaust fumes from automobiles.

The longest subway system in the world is in London, England (252 miles). But the busiest subway system is in New York City (237 miles). Though not as long as the London underground (the British term for

subway), it has about 200 more stations. The first subway started running in New York City in 1904. Boston, Washington, Atlanta, Moscow, Paris, Tokyo, and Mexico City are some of the other big cities with subway systems. One of the newest and quietest is the Bay Area Rapid Transit (BART) in San Francisco. There the track is mounted on rubber dampeners to deaden the noise as trains run along the track. The rails are welded together so that passengers don't hear any *click-clack* sound. BART trains are so quiet that you scarcely know when they glide in and out of a station.

Elevated Trains are the opposite of subways. Instead of traveling under city traffic, they speed along on overhead rails *above* the automobiles. One of the most famous elevated trains is the new Skytrain in Vancouver, Canada. Skytrain is only the sixth railway system in the world to operate without drivers. The cars do not have even a driver's front window. All of the trains are automatically controlled by computer systems. Passengers never see the computers or their operators, who remain in the control centers. The skytrain rails are mounted on giant concrete beams. Each car is powered by two electro-magnetic motors fitted underneath. The motors help to create a magnetic force that pulls the car along and stops it.

Monorails often travel overhead, too. The name monorail means there is just one rail. The train may travel on top of the rail, straddling it. Or the cars may hang from arms curving down from the rail. One well-known monorail runs through the zoo gardens of Ueno Park in Tokyo, Japan. Its rail section carries weight-supporting wheels on top, with balancing and driving wheels on the sides. The rubber tires on the wheels are responsible for the smooth ride.